Copies of this and other books
are available from the publisher at discount
when purchased in quantity
for boards of directors or staff.
Call 508-359-0019

FUNDRAISING MISTAKES THAT BEDEVIL ALL BOARDS (AND STAFF TOO)

A 1-Hour Guide
to Identifying and Overcoming
Obstacles to Your Success

First printed September 2004

10 9 8 7 6 5 4 3 2

Printed in the United States of America
This text is printed on acid-free paper.

Copies of this book are available from the
publisher at discount when purchased in
quantity for boards of directors or staff.

Emerson & Church, Publishers
P.O. Box 338 • Medfield, MA 02052
Tel. 508-359-0019 • Fax 508-359-2703
www.contributionsmagazine.com

Library of Congress Cataloging-in-Publication Data

Grace, Kay Sprinkel.
  Fundraising mistakes that bedevil all boards (and staff too)
: a 1-hour guide to identifying and overcoming obstacles to
your success / by Kay Sprinkel Grace.
     p. cm.
  ISBN 1-889102-22-9 (pbk. : alk. paper)
  1. Fund raising--United States. 2. Nonprofit organizations-
-United States--Finance. 3. Social service--United States--
Finance. I. Title.
  HV41.9.U5G713 2004
  361.7'63'0681--dc22
                                                    2004017487

Kay Sprinkel Grace

FUNDRAISING
MISTAKES THAT
BEDEVIL
ALL BOARDS
(AND STAFF TOO)

A 1-Hour Guide to
Identifying and
Overcoming
Obstacles to
Your Success

Emerson
& Church
PUBLISHERS

Also by Kay Sprinkel Grace

The Ultimate Board Member's Book:
A 1-Hour Guide to Understanding and Fulfilling
Your Role and Responsibilities
2003
ISBN 1-889102-18-0

Over Goal! What You Must Know
to Excel at Fundraising Today
2003
ISBN 1-889102-14-8

High Impact Philanthropy: How Donors,
Boards, and Nonprofit Organizations
Can Transform Communities
2000

Co-author with Alan Wendroff
ISBN 0-471-36918-7

Beyond Fund Raising: New Strategies for
Nonprofit Innovation and Investment
1997
ISBN 0471-16232-9

This book is dedicated to my mother,
who taught me that you cannot accomplish
great things if you are afraid to make a
mistake. At 96, she is still unafraid.

"Mistakes are the portals of discovery."

–James Joyce

CONTENTS

INTRODUCTION

In my decades of work with nonprofits, I have addressed many recurring mistakes that board members, volunteers, and staff make when raising money.

The "aha!" that occurs when we fix the mistake is so transforming I thought I'd like to capture the "Top 40" in this book.

Some mistakes are absolute (they are poor practice wherever you are and whatever you do); some are relative to your community or cause. If you find that only 35 of these apply to your situation, I believe you'll still find your fundraising improved.

My hope is that this book will be a useful tool for board members and staff alike. For board members, weary of lengthy training sessions or coaching, it will save you time.

As a guide for staff members just starting out, or those needing a boost in helping board members become more comfortable and effective in their fundraising role, its shortcut approach will be appealing.

Regardless of your role, I do hope what you're about to read will be informative, a bit fun, and, most importantly, helpful in advancing the cause to which you are committed.

San Francisco, Calif.   Kay Sprinkel Grace

1

MISTAKE

Tax deductibility is a powerful incentive

The tax advantages of giving are motivating for some. But for most, they aren't a prime incentive.

Ironically, the very people we think of as most needing a tax break are often maxed out on their deductions.

One generous donor to a major university, setting up an estate gift, was told of the sizable tax advantage involved. Her reply was that she'd have to live to be 120 to realize all of the accrued benefits from her philanthropy (she was in her 80s at the time!).

To be sure, you'll want to understand the donor's circumstances well enough to know the tax ramifications. And be prepared to speak to them if asked. But don't lead off with talk about the IRS, unless the prospect has given you reason to.

Virtually any nonprofit can offer the identical tax advantage. But not every organization can match the donor's values and dreams as yours can.

Seek out the donor's true motivation, in your conversations with her and by reviewing any information your organization has about her giving. And then speak to that motivation in your presentation. Only then will you stoke her desire to support you.

Incidentally, anecdotal research done several years ago showed that on a list of 25 reasons why people give, "tax concerns" was number 16.

2

MISTAKE

Foundation and corporations are the biggest donors

Gifts from foundations and corporations, unlike those from individuals, are often widely publicized. That's why Kresge and Bank of America, and other foundations and corporations like them, enjoy the reputation for being the best source of large gifts, and why we expend so much energy soliciting them.

But if you look closely at American philanthropy, you'll see that giving by foundations and corporations account for only 15 or so percent of all the money given each year to charitable organizations. The rest comes from individuals like you and me.

Even so, many board members will persist in believing that foundations and corporations are the roads to riches.

I, for one, think it's because grantseeking is typically spearheaded by staff who do the research, write the proposals, and follow up. Boards often defer to this kind of giving because, typically, they needn't get involved on a personal basis with asking.

But individuals are a vast and wonderful market. They don't have to consult a committee to make a gift. They can give without restrictions. They'll give more than once a year if so moved. They live in the community and are invested in the outcomes.

Don't overlook foundations and corporations, but focus your energy on individuals. The payoff will be far greater.

3

MISTAKE

Special events are the best way to raise money

At one time, special events seemed to be the best way to raise money. The blockbuster gala, netting $50,000, struck everyone as a quick fix for the annual fund.

The problem, we came to see later, was that most of our net figures didn't include "soft costs" like staff time. When these and other expenses were factored in, the net plummeted.

Regrettably, the lesson hasn't been learned by enough organizations. Calendars in most communities are so full that caring people could be at three events a week and, during the spring and fall, three events a night! One friend recently termed the event we were attending part of her "100 Days in May."

In my first job, I inherited a calendar in which there were nine events of modest scale (domino tournament, tennis tournament) and one blockbuster (a summer symphony concert). In my youthful zeal, I added another big wine tasting party.

Then came our sobering year-end cost analysis. Not only was our net much lower than reported, but volunteer burnout (even with a large auxiliary) was spreading like a virus. So was staff burnout. Gradually we scaled back and began expanding our outreach to individuals for major gifts.

We keep falling into the special events trap for two reasons. They prevent us from having to approach our friends and colleagues for significant gifts (we can sell them tickets or a table, instead). And – from the outside – they appear quick and easy. Put together an event. Open the doors. Have a good time. Count the money.

But if you've ever chaired an event, you know how deceptive that is. You're better served devoting the same amount of time to cultivating those who can make large gifts.

View special events primarily as "friend raisers." Then your expectations will be much more realistic.

4

MISTAKE

People will give just because yours is a good cause

I wish this were true. Just think how strong our community organizations would be and how much less time we'd have to spend raising money.

But, alas, yours can be the best cause in the world and still not raise money if:

1) You fail to involve the right people

2) You neglect the 'harder' side of your mission: namely, delivering results in a cost-effective way.

In all but the extraordinary case (the plight of a desperate child who makes front page news comes to mind) the *people* involved with the cause determine its ability to raise money.

An old fundraising adage still rings true: "People don't give to causes, they give to people who believe in causes."

Unless you, your CEO and staff, and your volunteers are committed to the mission, communicate its importance, and develop relationships with those who share your values, you won't attract substantial or long-lasting support.

But that's only part of the story. You still need an organization with integrity, that's well-run, whose impact can be quantified.

Today's donors are a demanding lot. Unless you meet these criteria, they'll simply go shopping for another organization that does.

5

MISTAKE

Donors are drawn to organizations in need

Decades ago, when the nonprofit playing field was less crowded, many people responded to an organization's neediness.

Some of our organizations even portrayed themselves this way: shabby offices, amateurish publications, and seat of the pants financing.

All that has changed. Those who lament that money pours into great universities, major arts organizations, and other giant nonprofit enterprises rather than to those who really "need" it have to see the reason why: these organizations smell of success. They are professional, accountable, good at reporting their impact, and offer opportunities for people to fulfill their charitable instincts *and* have their investment protected.

A message of desperation may work once. Or even twice. But some great community orchestras in the 80s and 90s finally slipped off the horizon when their frantic plea for money began to fall on deaf ears. Those who had bailed them out let loose of the bucket.

Years ago I spoke of our need to put away the tin cup. To stop begging. But, unfortunately, the mentality still lingers, in part because the very origins of many of our organizations were based on presenting themselves as charities in need of a handout.

We must move away from that.

Present your organization for what it is – dedicated, robust, visionary, making a difference in the community. Donors will be drawn to you. I guarantee it.

6

MISTAKE

You can secure big gifts by writing letters

This is one of the biggest mistakes board members make and it happens all the time.

In fact, I recently heard of a letter asking for $3 million. Imagine. It seems the relationship between the asker and the asked was too strained for a personal meeting!

I'm not saying it can't be done. And there are instances when a letter is the right approach.

But for the most part big gifts are sought in person. The actual moment of asking is the end result of research, cultivation, dialog, shared values, and – most importantly – the creation of a relationship.

Yet we persist in writing letters for a number of reasons.

First, and perhaps foremost, it means we don't have to put ourselves on the line, and face the possibility of rejection or embarassment.

Second, many people insist they can present the case more effectively in a letter (in which case it should be used as a warm-up for the visit with the prospective donor).

Third – and perhaps the only reason that justifies a letter – are circumstances that make a letter the only option: schedules, geography, illness, or the prospective donor *demands* the request in writing. But the fact that you know these conditions means you've had communication with either the prospect or her representative. That is critical.

If you're tempted to write a letter because you feel clumsy about asking or don't want to face possible rejection, work to overcome your own feelings and misgivings.

Ask for coaching. Ask for a partner to go with you. But don't jeopardize your cause by capitulating to your own fears.

7

MISTAKE

Publicity raises money

Too often, we believe that just spreading the word will solve our funding problems. People will read about the good things we're doing and – bingo! – they'll send in fistfuls of dollars.

One organization I worked with was featured in a national magazine in which one of the people interviewed cited the amount needed for a new facility. The organization honestly expected to be flooded with gifts as a result. It didn't happen. A few gifts trickled in, but no significant outpouring.

Publicity is essential in building an image in the community. But it shouldn't be relied on as an avenue for fundraising. They are separate functions.

Raising awareness of your impact and the credibility of your organization is critical. Bus and bus shelter ads, articles in newspapers and magazines, PSAs, billboard advertising – all contribute to your brand recognition. To the extent you can get such support on a pro bono basis, all the better.

But marketing does little more than pave the way for fundraising. You still have to get out there and ask.

In fact, it is only when an individual you're soliciting says to you, "I'm making this gift because I recently read about your work," that you know your publicity has been effective.

8

People dislike giving

Although they may balk at the amount of the request or need a "gestation" period before agreeing to invest, most people do like to give. In fact, most express a feeling of true joy when giving.

Those new to fundraising think it's all about pressure, about talking someone into a gift they don't want to make. But in fact pressure doesn't really work or, at best, works one time and ultimately creates ill will. You can bet you'll be shunned if you use hard-sell tactics.

Now it is true that some don't like to be *asked*. Usually these are people who aren't interested in or linked to your organization, who feel that your asking is an invasion of their privacy, or worry that if they give they'll be besieged by others as well.

But the reluctance of most of these individuals can be overcome if we work to improve the way we ask, and focus on the prospect's needs and interests while building a relationship.

As I'll reiterate throughout this book, don't second-guess a person's intentions. Too often we arbitrarily decide not to ask someone because we're sure they don't like to give.

Instead, assume that most people enjoy giving. You just have to inspire them by asking in the right way.

9

MISTAKE

Big donors are different, they're not like us

I often alter a quote from the lexicon of that great American philosopher, Pogo the Possum (a creation of the late cartoonist, Walt Kelly), who said, "We have met the enemy, and he is us." My version is: "We have met the donor, and he (or she) is us."

Giving cuts across all demographics. The people we approach are in fact a lot like us: many live next door, are in our kids' carpool, compete on the same golf course, and are waiting in line next to you. Ironically, some of them may look at us and want to bring us closer to an organization they care about.

Even those who do live in the gated community on the other side of town, or the penthouse apartment on the lake, still have common connecting points with us. They care about the same things, feel the same pain over a loss, and want to be part of the solution to a chronic community problem.

If, for example, I'm a board member from the middle class fighting to eradicate leukemia, and your daughter has been diagnosed with the disease, exactly how important is it that my financial assets pale next to yours?

We share the hope to end this scourge; it is what draws us together despite our socioeconomic disparity.

Giving is a matter of the heart, and is inspired when reputable organizations connect with people who care. Reaching out to them with an invitation to make a difference, to join with you in combating a disease or building a school, will be the bridge between you and people from all corners of your community.

10

MISTAKE

We can't raise big money, we don't know any rich people

I once oversaw a church campaign for $12 million in a woefully impoverished area. It was clear from the outset that none of the people involved knew anyone wealthy.

But we didn't let that stop us.

Through a carefully developed plan that engaged the board as well as a community committee, we identified people who cared about the church's work, its pastor, and the parishioners. And they responded generously – one individual gave $1 million – because they shared our values.

We limit ourselves when we think that because we're a small organization, or serve a limited population, few will be interested.

But it isn't the size of the organization that matters, it's the importance of the mission. When Project Open Hand was launched, an organization that brings meals to homebound people with HIV/AIDS, it was from the kitchen of the founder and the meals were delivered in friends' cars.

Although the group was tiny, and the founder didn't know many wealthy individuals, support poured in. Why? The need was great, and Project Open Hand was meeting it. The word got out, and people invested.

You don't need wealthy people in your data base to raise money. But without them, there are two imperatives facing you:

1) You must get your message out and relate the impact of what you're doing to the broader needs of the community, and

2) You must be willing to think of ways to identify and approach those who do have money.

In the case of the church, their work with the poor and indigent, as well as the large ethnic communities in the neighborhood, was attractive to the million-dollar donor whose own family, decades ago, had been a struggling immigrant family attending the church. The community had changed as had the origin of the immigrants, but the donor saw that the church and its mission and people were worthy of his investment.

If you don't know wealthy people, make no mistake: raising money is much harder and demands more imagination. But it is not impossible. With dedication – and tenacity – on the part of the board and the staff it can be done.

11

MISTAKE

Giving is largely a rational decision

If there's any transaction that engages the left and right brain more fully than making a charitable investment, I don't know of it.

Lean too strongly to one lobe or the other, and you jeopardize the gift.

Plans, budgets, blueprints, architectural models – these all appeal to a donor's rational side. They give comfort. They show your foundation is solid – and that's important.

But even the best laid plans, in and of themselves, won't elicit a gift. The donor has to feel an emotional tug as well. In his heart, he has to identify with your dreams and vision.

That's why it's always important to seek a balance when approaching donors. Support your stories by statistics, and your statistics with stories.

If, for example, you tell a donor you served 600 families last year, tell her about one of those families. Or, if you start by describing one of those families, be sure to let the donor know the story was played out 600 times in different ways.

Because so many organizations have abused the emotional side of giving (direct mailings with bashed baby seals, vivisected animals, starving children) countless people have numbed themselves to exploitative appeals. Who can blame them?

But there is always a place for genuine emotion, especially as ours is the business of improving and often saving lives.

Share your success stories and even a hardened rationalist can soften.

12

MISTAKE

Others are more comfortable asking for money than you

Everyone thinks this. Others make it look so easy. But, believe me, they have the same anxieties as you.

There's nothing in the way most of us were raised that prepared us for asking for money. From the anxiety we felt as children beseeching our parents for a dollar or two more, to the discomfort we've all experienced when pressed for a loan by friends or relatives in a pinch, we find such transactions innately distasteful.

Further, many of us were reared to believe it's a sign of weakness to ask – and we still harbor this feeling when we set about soliciting gifts.

Perhaps the problem is this: we see ourselves begging for money for a needy cause rather than offering an opportunity to invest in an organization that's addressing important needs in the community.

But offering a life-enriching opportunity is precisely what we're doing, and it's imperative to adopt this perspective.

In all the years I've asked for money, I still get butterflies before making a call. Once I'm into it, particularly if I'm with another board member, that discomfort fades. But it comes right back before my next call.

So expect the flutters. Just don't let them weaken your resolve.

13

MISTAKE

The state of the economy is key to fundraising

Even when times are bad, we shouldn't second-guess whether someone will give. The late Hank Rosso, great teacher of philanthropy and mentor to many, said we should never deny anyone the right to say no ... or yes.

He was right.

The stock market could be sagging, earnings soft, inventories swelling, but still you ask. Why? For two reasons:

1) You can't make valid assumptions about someone else's financial situation, and

2) The individual may be *more* embarrassed by not being asked (especially when

he learns his friends and colleagues have been) than by having to say no or give a smaller gift.

If people care deeply about an issue, they'll often find a way to support it. Maybe not at the level you had hoped, but frequently they will come through.

When deciding whether to give, a donor considers a range of factors. Among them are: the integrity of the organization, her link to it, the passion she feels for the cause, the "return" she's received on a previous investment, and the ability of the asker to convey the urgency of giving now.

Certainly the state of the economy, and the investments in a personal portfolio, influence the decision to give. But by no means do they dictate it.

14

MISTAKE

Men and women are alike in their giving

Although the differences between men's and women's giving have lessened, they do still exist.

For example, most women tend to look for partnership and engagement in their giving. For them, it's not about the transaction – it's what happens afterwards that's important. They want a relationship, not just recognition.

Also, women's giving is often motivated by something highly personal. Recently, I met a woman who has single-handedly created a fund to address a debilitating disease that afflicts her child. She has taken up the standard and is raising money and visibility for the disease that was all but ignored.

Then too, women like to be asked in a way that recognizes their own income or assets, and acknowledges their role in making giving decisions in their families.

But there's something else you should know about gender differences. It appears that 21st Century philanthropy is not your father's philanthropy – it's more like your mother's.

Traditionally, men have practiced "checkbook" philanthropy, based largely on peer pressure to give and the notion that writing a check fulfilled a responsibilty to the community.

Women, on the other hand, have always wanted and needed involvement before giving at any significant level. Women will volunteer, get involved, give, get more involved, give more – a wonderful progressive cycle that can last a lifetime.

If not completely moribund, checkbook philanthropy is on its last legs. For a host of reasons, fundraising abuses being one of them, today's donors are increasingly involved in the organizations they support and insistent on accountability.

15

MISTAKE

Wealth is mostly what determines a person's willingness to give

When an individual makes a philanthropic gift, at least three factors come into play: He or she has:

- A connection to the organization
- Concern for the cause
- The financial capacity to give

It may surprise you that the first two far outweigh the third. A person can have incalculable wealth, but if she's not connected to the people or services of your organization or doesn't display interest in what you're doing, she's not likely to give.

I know of one organization that wined

and dined a man with huge financial resources, hoping for a lead gift. He had a
known interest in the kind of work the group
did, and he had assets.

But he didn't have a connection to the organization, nor was there much evidence he
placed a value on philanthropy.

After months of negotiations the wooing
came to an end. "No dice," the man finally
said. Time was wasted and, even worse, the
person who ultimately did step forward with
the lead gift felt ignored during the process.

I probably see this mistake more than any
other. Someone will excitedly hand me a list
– of potential donors, of people to interview
for a feasibility study, of individuals to invite
to a particular function. When I ask how
these are connected to the organization, more
often than not the answer is 'they aren't.'

Too often, as a starting point, board and
staff members will scribble down the names
of wealthy people in the community. Give
that up. Instead, list only the people you
know who share your organization's values.
Not only will they be more responsive, they'll
also be willing to link you to others (perhaps
with more money) who care about what you
do.

16

MISTAKE

To secure a gift, saying just the right words is key

If this were true, we could all carry the same script when calling upon prospects and be done with it. We could all use the same foundation or corporation proposals. And all fundraising letters would be nearly identical.

While there are certain things you should say and do because we know they work, even these can be set aside if you have a better way of saying the same thing and getting the right result.

The only "right words" are those that reflect you and the organization, and those you know are "right" for the donor because you've been a good listener and discerned what she cares about.

Are there formulas? Of course. In direct mail the simplest one I know is: touch my heart, tell me what the problem is, tell me what you're doing about it, and tell me how I can help. But those aren't the words – that is the framework.

Grant proposals also have a structure that should be followed, usually provided by the potential funder. But the way you fill in the blanks with your passion and programs is critical.

As for what to say when calling upon a prospective donor, that depends on the two of you. Remember, you're having a conversation – it has to feel natural.

The best advice is perhaps the simplest – be yourself. Say what feels comfortable for you. And accept that the words won't always flow.

One volunteer, intimidated by a prospect she was calling on who was older and in a higher position in the same company, finally asked the man for the gift – $25,000. He seemed stunned, and said no one had ever asked him for a gift that size. She blurted out the first thing that came to her mind: "Well, I've never ASKED anyone for a gift that size." They both laughed … and he made the gift.

17

MISTAKE

You don't have to give in order to ask others to give – your time is your gift

This mistaken belief continues to plague board leaders and development officers as they work to ensure that *every* member of the board makes an annual gift or a pledge to the campaign.

For generations, there was perhaps a belief on the part of many board members and volunteers that time and money were interchangeable. But that day is long past.

Now donors – individuals as well as foundations and corporations – routinely ask about the level of board support. Some even want to know what percentage of the board has contributed and what the aggregate giving is. To respond that your board gives its time no longer satisfies.

But there's another key reason why you have to reach into your own pocket: you can't effectively ask for a gift until you've given yourself.

Donors are wise. They'll often question you about your own support. If you, who are closest to the organization, haven't made a financial commitment, your appeal to them is an empty one. "Come back when you've decided what *you're* going to give," they'll sometimes say.

As a board member, you should expect to be asked for an annual or capital gift in a personal meeting with the board chair and CEO. Only then – in the context of your service being acknowledged and your ongoing role in the organization discussed – will the request for your gift be like the one you'll eventually make of others.

You, too, deserve to experience the joy of giving.

18

MISTAKE

It's impolite to ask for a specific amount

It troubles many people to ask for a specified amount.

They believe it reveals to the donor that they've gathered a lot of personal information about him (net worth, real estate holdings, giving history, gifts to other organizations). They also balk at putting the number out there, fearing it'll cause surprise, resentment, or anger.

But step aside for a moment, and look at it from the donor's perspective. If you've approached things right, the person on whom you're calling is acquainted with your organization, knows the purpose of your visit, and has agreed to meet with you.

Probably the biggest unknown, as far as the donor is concerned, is just how much you're seeking.

I've been on calls when someone on our team will (regrettably) say, "And so, Charlie, we hope you'll consider being part of this effort to build a community theater and that you'll make a significant gift." Significant gift. What does that mean? $5,000? $50,000? $500,000?

You need to cite a specific amount – or, if not an exact amount, at least a range. Otherwise you leave the prospect in the uncomfortable position of having to divine what you want.

Most capital campaigns (and many annual campaigns too) use either a gift range chart or a list of naming opportunities ("For a gift of $1 million, this facility will bear the name of your loved one").

Some askers, uncomfortable with putting forth a figure, will hand the chart to the prospect. "We were hoping you'd consider making a leadership gift in the range of $10,000 to $25,000." Not as good as asking for $25,000 outright, but better than being vague.

Be forewarned, however – the prospect will lean toward the lower figure if you haven't inspired him with the cause.

Be as specific as you can with your request. Rather than be resentful, your prospect will likely respect that you've done your homework.

19

MISTAKE

Asking once a year is enough

Decades ago, when I was first involved as a volunteer in Stanford University fundraising, I served on what was called the Creative Committee. We were a group of alums with experience in marketing and fundraising who advised the annual fund office on its mailings.

I remember how we prided ourselves on our fall campaign letter – usually signed by the university president – promising that if an alum gave when the letter was received (usually in September), he wouldn't hear from us or be "bothered again" until the following September.

I shudder to remember that. It conveyed, first, that asking and giving were a "bother," and second that we only cared to contact our alums when we wanted money.

Fortunately, this is long in Stanford's past. But I see the practice repeated in organizations that are newer to fundraising. Because we believe people feel put upon when asked, we want to keep the irritation as low as possible.

What we fail to understand is the joy our donors feel when giving, all the more enhanced when we can show the impact of their past and current gifts.

Even though a donor's gift may have been recent, we can still let her know that as successful as our tutoring program is, we've identified 40 more eligible students who are now on a waiting list. Is this something she'd be willing to help us with?

Over the years, one of the benefits I've found in engaging volunteers in thankathons is the power of hearing a donor say how much it means to be able to give. It turns out that giving isn't a bother at all.

Ask because you are succeeding, not because you need money. And ask more than once because your programs are growing ... as is your impact in the community.

20

MISTAKE

Development staff, because it's their job, are more effective in asking

Although many universities and other larger institutions have converted to staff-only fundraising, it's a mistake in my view.

While development staff may be more "effective" from the standpoint of being thoroughly trained in asking, and having at their disposal a reservoir of facts and information about the organization, still these advantages pale in comparison to what you offer.

First, as a board member, you bring a particular passion and perspective to the table based on your decision to become involved.

It is not your paying job. You don't have to show up. But the fact that you do lends great credibility to the organization you represent.

Second, fundraising isn't about personal eloquence or asking in a perfect way. It's about relationships and respect and influence. It is the rare staff person who travels in the same social circles as his prospective donors.

Finally, in the mind of the would-be donor, a development officer is paid to ask. In fact, his livelihood is tied up with getting a 'yes.' You on the other hand are in the irreproachable position of having nothing to gain from your visit except the satisfaction of furthering a cause you believe in.

You are every bit as effective in asking as the development officer (at least in my opinion). And, as a team, the two of you are virtually unstoppable.

And speaking of teamwork, there's sometimes a mistaken notion that with a good development director, the board can be less involved in fundraising.

In fact the opposite is true. With a skilled development director, expect to be *more* engaged in fundraising.

I've heard board members say – often at

the beginning of a search process – that they can hardly wait to hire a development director so they can get some rest from all the fundraising.

I quickly counsel that any professional worth her salt will expect (and implicitly demand) a board that's fully committed to donor relations and fundraising.

Great development directors are choreographers, conductors, and facilitators. They provide structure, offer training, develop materials, give direction, and often accompany board members on certain calls.

A development director is a partner, one who assigns, prods, cajoles, cheerleads, and keeps things organized.

But he or she can't succeed without you and your wholehearted commitment.

21

MISTAKE

Fundraising consultants (and development officers) often bring with them lists of people to solicit

A colleague of mine, who had worked at a major cultural organization during its capital campaign, was recently hired by another organization.

When she arrived on the job, the board and CEO said, "Well, where's the list?" My friend was incredulous. At first, she thought they were kidding. But, they were unrelenting that she hand over the list of people who had contributed to the university's campaign. After a few months, she resigned.

Carrying a list of prospects from one

organization to another is a breach of fundraising ethics. Why? Because the individuals on the list have relationships with the organization that have been developed over time. Traveling lists would be a practice that treats donors like a commodity instead of as investors motivated by mission and shared values.

Are there exceptions to the rule? None that I can think of. But there are acceptable practices that can draw on a consultant's knowledge.

For example, if in your database there's a prospect being actively cultivated, and it's someone with whom the consultant has worked in another organization, it is perfectly ethical for her to offer insights, comments, and strategies based on her knowledge of the person.

It is also within the ethical code for a consultant, in reviewing *your* list of potential prospects, to comment on her experience with someone on the list.

But don't expect consultants or new staff to bring lists with them from another organization. Not only will you be disappointed, but it's likely your own ethics will be called into question.

22

MISTAKE

We can run this campaign on the cheap

One of my early lessons in fund development was that you have to spend money to make money. Yet, so many organizations still struggle with this reality.

Board members and CFOs often try to stint on both "soft" and "hard" costs.

One organization, preparing for a *several hundred million dollar* campaign, asked their CFO to challenge a relatively small expense I (as the consultant) had recommended for "cultivation."

Only after I went through a lengthy explanation of why people had to be cultivated before they could be asked for six and seven-figure gifts did the CFO agree and recommend that the board back down.

Another so-called soft item that's neglected is training. I've known boards to limp along in their solicitations because they refused to hire a trainer to help them learn the way to state the case and handle objections.

But hard items such as materials and personnel aren't spared either. I've seen campaign brochures so amateurish they lacked all credibility. I've also come into organizations where development staffing levels were so bare bones people were fatigued, angry, and devoid of any motivation.

Clearly, you must contain the costs of fundraising – this isn't the place for extravagance. But penny-pinching a campaign's infrastructure will eventually backfire.

You'd be smarter to delay your campaign than to starve it.

23

MISTAKE

You need a powerful board to have a successful campaign

There are organizations across America – particularly universities, hospitals and large arts and cultural organizations – whose boards are the envy of all.

The people on these boards are leaders in commerce, industry, education, and possess wealth and connections in abundance.

Annually they provide leadership gifts of six and even seven figures. And during times of a capital campaign, their gifts often constitute as much as 80 percent of the total goal.

If this doesn't sound like your board, well ... join the club. For every organization so blessed, there are thousands upon thousands with boards more like yours.

These organizations are governed by people who care deeply about the mission, share what wealth and connections they have, and are willing to work to fulfill the vision. And many excel.

Even if yours isn't a 'power' board, you can still have a successful campaign.

Probably the most common alternative is to form a campaign cabinet or steering committee that engages a few members of the board as well as high-profile leaders from the community.

I've found that while many 'movers and shakers' may not care to join the board, or be involved on a sustained basis, they will participate in a time-limited campaign, assuming they have some passion for the project.

A food bank I know of used this model for its capital campaign and surpassed its goal. Religious organizations have used the same approach with great success. And social service organizations often form campaign leadership organizations that involve both board and non-board volunteers.

Power is a relative concept. Enlist the right people, even if they're not on your board, and suddenly your organization too has the power to mount a successful campaign.

24

Not everyone on the board has to be involved in fundraising

Everyone on the board *has* to be involved in raising money, but not everyone has to ASK. Leaving the asking to a committee is frequently done; but no sensible organization leaves board members out of the full "development" process.

Let me clarify. There is a difference between development and fundraising. Development is the process of identifying and cultivating potential donors, and maintaining relationships once these individuals have given. Fundraising focuses on the actual asking.

It is the responsibility of the entire board

to be involved in development, while it's possible that only selected members can be involved in asking.

One board member I worked with insisted she would "do anything but ask for money," a common refrain. I asked how she'd like to help. "Well, I know lots of people," she informed me, "and have good lists."

This was indeed the case.

We used her lists extensively when we held our cultivation events. And, when all was said and done, nearly a quarter of all the money raised came from donors she directed us to.

You don't have to ask for a gift to be involved in raising money. You simply have to accept responsibility for assisting in the most productive way you can.

25

MISTAKE

It's prudent to focus on large donors only

Anyone who contributes to your cause is interested in it and has the potential to become more involved, whether by giving again or participating in another way.

By focusing only on those who give large gifts, you send a signal that money is your only interest. What you lose sight of is the following:

1) *Anyone, no matter the size of his gift, can become a champion for you.* Astute organizations understand this. Particularly during economic downturns, they engage people in other ways, realizing that the size of their gift doesn't really reflect the overall potential.

One symphony orchestra I'm familiar with actually brought in more money and more donors during an economic slump by letting smaller givers know how valuable they were.

The organization took the further step of engaging their younger subscribers in various activities, essentially sending the message that they cared about those who cared about them. It worked.

2) *Giving according to one's means should be respected.* What about the donor for whom a gift of $100 represents a greater share of income than another's gift of $1,000? Do we minimize the gift and dishonor her commitment?

As our society ages, more and more people are on fixed incomes. They deserve our outreach, not only for the obvious potential of estate gifts, but also because many are alone and our contact gives them joy. Let us not lose sight that the historic meaning of the word philanthropy, is 'love of people.'

3) *Many a donor puts his toe in the water first.* Often a donor will test an organization with a small gift, withholding a larger sum until he sees how his small gift is acknowledged, what use it is put to, and what

further overtures will be made.

Countless 'angel investors' have moved on to other organizations after being ignored by those preoccupied by large donors.

Reach as deeply into your donor base as you can with your gratitude. Not only will you communicate a great deal about your organization's values, you'll create legions of new champions as well.

26

MISTAKE

Estate gifts only come from big donors

If there's one mistake that's being chal-
lenged daily, it is this one. We read all the
time about the $25 donor who bequeaths $1
million to the local animal shelter, or the de-
cades-lapsed donor whose estate provides
hundreds of thousands of dollars to an organization in which she or her husband was
once active.

Museums and other membership organizations are getting smart about this – look-
ing to members, docents, and other volunteers as well as steady donors of $100 or less,
and educating them about the possibility of
simple bequests and other deferred giving

options.

One nonprofit I know worked with a loyal volunteer, a retired school teacher, to help her see how her estate could benefit the organization. She put her modest house in a trust. When she died years later, the property values in her community had soared. Her house, for which she paid $10,000, commanded more than a half million dollars.

Yet, this woman's annual gift had never exceeded $100.

27

You need a stable of annual donors to have a successful capital campaign

Certainly, it's easier to conduct a capital campaign if you have a large group of annual donors. But don't make the mistake of thinking you absolutely need them to raise big money.

Even established organizations with relatively small annual giving programs have been successful at capital campaigns.

For example, the food bank I mentioned earlier had a limited number of annual donors. But because of the organization's visibility (it had conducted food drives in locations throughout the community), and because of its reputation, the group was able to convince would-be donors that a new facility was needed. People invested at high levels.

Start-up organizations often seek capital funding long before they have a base of annual donors. An independent high school in Southern California raised $34 million for the initial phase of its buildings – two years before the school enrolled its first student or started an annual fund. The promise was great, the values were clear, and the community rallied to help create this new opportunity for its young people.

It's important to build a strong annual giving program – for lots of reasons. But, if you've never attracted many annual donors or are just starting out, don't be discouraged.

With a bold vision and a committed inner corps, you can raise the money you need.

28

If you don't know how much a prospect can give, shoot for the moon

In a way it's flattering to be asked for a large gift, even when we can't afford it (we all like to appear prosperous, it seems).

But that doesn't mean you should ask for an unsupportable amount.

Vastly overreaching a person's capacity makes you look foolish and arouses doubts about your organization's credibility. This goes for corporations and foundations as well.

If a donor has never given you more than $1,000 and her largest capital gift to *any* cause was $25,000, you will err – and perhaps embarrass or rankle her – by asking for $100,000 unless there's some recent circumstance (inheritance, for instance) that has changed her capacity to give.

But let me quickly add a cautionary note: don't ask for too little either. If someone has a philanthropic pattern of giving at a certain level, don't lowball your request because of certain assumptions you've made ("That new addition cost plenty"). You'll get the low amount. Quickly.

Instead, strike the right place based on research and first-hand knowledge of the person's wealth and giving potential.

Stretch is good – unrealistic ask is not.

29

MISTAKE

Some people can't afford to give and shouldn't be asked

I have sat at boardroom tables for years, reviewing lists with board members, and over and over I hear:

- "Oh, they can't give. They don't have any money."
- "Them? They're paying off a pledge to their university – forget it." Or,
- "They're tapped out with their daughter's wedding."

But second-guessing whether someone can give only invites problems. You risk offending the donor (who may in fact want to be asked) and miss the opportunity of connecting the person to your organization even if she can't give right now.

Years ago, when I was the volunteer chair for a national campaign, my steering committee and I hit the fourth year of a five-year campaign and, in truth, we were exhausted.

We debated whether to continue soliciting in a very personal way, or to surrender some prospects to a more generic approach. We even discussed whether it was necessary to call upon everyone if we reached our goal beforehand.

One of our steering committee members told a story that inspired us to soldier on. In her home city there had been a recent dedication of a new cultural center. With her husband away, she invited a friend to accompany her. The friend hesitated and said she wasn't interested. Sensing a problem, my colleague gently probed. It turns out the women was resentful because no one had ever asked her for a gift to the new center, and she felt their campaign leadership had made an assumption she couldn't give.

This sobering story helped us stay the course, exceed our goal, and cover more than 90 percent of our assigned prospects.

Never assume someone can't give.

30

MISTAKE

You need a feasibility study before launching a capital campaign

A feasibility study, in which board and community representatives are queried about an organization's image, its visibility in the community, its proposed campaign, and the likelihood of the interviewee contributing, used to be standard preparation for a capital or endowment drive. Increasingly, organizations are going forward without such a study.

The reasons vary. For instance, some organizations understand full well that no matter what the study shows, they must proceed anyway. The school has to be expanded. The roof needs to be replaced. The birthing unit must be built.

Other agencies, having delayed their campaign due to a previous study's recommendation, feel they have enough information now to go forward.

Still other organizations consider the cost of a study, usually between $15,000 and $50,000, prohibitive, and are convinced they'll succeed without one.

Lastly, more and more organizations are identifying leadership gifts in the early planning stages of their campaign, thereby removing one of the key purposes of a feasibility study. They are talking directly to the prospects, getting their buy-in on the campaign from the very beginning.

Whether your organization conducts a feasibility study is up to you. But it would be a mistake to think your success hinges on one.

31

MISTAKE

If you've been trained in asking at one organization, you don't need to attend another agency's training

While the training at the natural history museum may have been stellar, and though many of the principles will transfer to the youth symphony, you still need to be trained in how to ask for the youth symphony.

When I conduct a board training or coaching session, I often hear that certain people aren't attending because they already know how to ask. That may be true – they may be skilled solicitors – but there are things particular to each organization that affect how you ask.

You are vulnerable to a great deal of discomfort if you don't get organization-specific training.

For example, you need 'Talking Points,' a list of the compelling reasons why the organization merits support.

You need to hear what the common objections are and how to respond to them.

You need stories and statistics you can use to inform your prospects, as well as information about budgets, the cost of fundraising, and how your endowment (if any) is managed.

Then too, you'll get your best practice in asking for this particular organization, using a script.

If all that isn't enough, one last advantage of attending the training is to get to know your fellow solicitors better. You just might identify the ideal person to team up with to make your calls more comfortable and more effective.

32

MISTAKE

For those giving small gifts, a simple acknowledgment is fitting

If this isn't the biggest mistake I'll cite in these pages, it's a close runner-up.

When deciding which donors to focus on, size does seem to matter for most organizations. The more a donor gives, the more an organization invests in him with respect to tangible gifts, appreciation lunches, and special privileges.

Seldom are donors at modest levels (say $25 or less) given more than perfunctory thanks. And even less frequently are they evaluated for their future giving potential (with the result that great donors often languish in the 'auto-receipt' pile).

What a missed opportunity.

At any level, people should be thanked personally for their gifts. One effective way is to organize a quarterly or biannual 'Thankathon," during which board and volunteers call every donor (yes, every donor) and thank them.

This can be a highly productive event for several reasons:

1) Thankathons tangibly show donors how much you value them. Not many organizations take the trouble to make these calls. That yours does will be remembered by the donor.

2) Thankathons can tell you a great deal about your supporters. Often donors are forthcoming about why they're giving, what initially piqued their interest, and may even offer constructive feedback about your organization.

3) Thankathons can quell fears about asking. Donors will often express how pleased they are to help. When a caller hears this, it validates that people *do* like to give. That's why participating in a thankathon is often the

first step toward a caller agreeing to solicit others.

Whether you thank with a printed card, a phone call, or a formal note, remember this is just the beginning. Stay connected. It's the only way to build a relationship with the donor and earn his loyalty and lasting support.

33

MISTAKE

If a donor is contributing to an organization similar to yours, asking her to give to you is poaching

Always keep in mind that philanthropy is driven by issues and values, not by organizations and their needs.

If a person cares deeply about music in the schools, for example, and is already giving to an organization with this mission, she is in fact the most likely prospect to give to another organization with the same goal. It is not either/or, it is both/and.

While institutional loyalty (a person's college, prep school, place of worship) still commands part of a person's philanthropy, we see increasingly that people invest in similar organizations because they want a particular need fulfilled or problem solved.

Those who support one environmental organization gravitate toward others; people supporting one museum invariably contribute to others in the community; those drawn to cancer research or homeless issues are known to support multiple organizations with related purposes.

If you worry about "poaching" donors from other organizations, don't think you have the power. The person you approach decides for himself where to direct his philanthropy.

If you like, encourage him to support your cause in addition to others. But in the end, it's his decision not yours. All you are doing is presenting the opportunity.

34

Your goal in a major gifts or capital campaign is simply the amount of money you need

Success in a capital or endowment campaign shouldn't be measured in dollars alone.

There are four purposes for any sizable campaign: raise the money, raise the organization's visibility, increase the pool of donors, and move the organization to the next level of performance.

Raising the money is clearly the primary purpose. Every person involved must be committed to, and willing to work toward, achieving the financial goal.

Raising visibility is a second aim. A successful campaign allows you to widely disseminate your message and reach people who currently aren't on your radar screen but may support your efforts in the future.

Engaging more donors is a third goal of a large campaign, as these intensive bursts tend to be inclusive of all types and sizes of donors.

Finally, taking the organization to the next level of excellence is the ultimate objective of any campaign. It is, after all, the reason you're raising money in the first place.

Campaigns are hard work. No doubt about it. But strangely enough, when you understand a campaign's full range of benefits, raising the money becomes just a little bit easier.

35

MISTAKE

Consultants aren't needed if you have a fundraising staff

Too often, board members hesitate to hire a consultant, believing staff can do everything. But as with any business, there are times when a consultant's perspective is not only useful, it's required.

There are at least three jobs that call for the objective perspective and special expertise of a consultant. They are:

1. *Campaign Feasibility Study*. This must be done by an outsider if the results are to be credible. These interviews with board members and others who represent the community, are more candid and confidential if

conducted by someone unaffiliated with the organization.

2. *Strategic Planning*. Whether for the development department or for the entire organization, overseeing this often lengthy process is best left to an outsider – someone free to challenge, stretch, and ignite the thinking of the board and staff.

3. *Development Audit*. This unbiased review of your fundraising practices and performance is an important periodic checkup for improving and adjusting the ways in which you raise money.

When staff requests approval for a consultant, there are usually legitimate reasons. Listen to them. Not only will a consultant relieve internal pressure, he or she can provide an external, objective perspective on your organization's next best step.

36

MISTAKE

Nowadays, people want you to get to the point and ask – cultivation wastes time

This mistake is sometimes made by those on the board who don't want cultivation themselves – they're ready to give, impatient to be asked, and don't want to waste time in what they sometimes call "the dance."

Often these are young people with new wealth. And chances are they've done their own research on the potential donors they want to approach.

Or, they may be "old school" fundraising volunteers – ones steeped in the tradition of philanthropy. They have all served on boards and, owing to a sense of noblesse oblige, routinely support each other's causes.

But, excepting these two very specific types, it's a good practice to assume that people like to be cultivated. They want to get to know you, understand what your organization is about, and learn how they can be involved.

If you approach them prematurely, they'll often turn you down or give much less than you had hoped for.

Having said that, it's important to understand that philanthropy today must be flexible enough to accommodate the differing styles of donors drawn to the promise of doing something meaningful in their communities.

While it's safe to assume people still want what has been called the 'institutional hug,' don't press your style on them. Find out what they need in terms of cultivation. Talk to staff. Talk to their friends. Best of all, engage the potential donor and listen to what he himself prefers.

37

MISTAKE

If your early fundraising calls don't spark interest, chances are you'll fail

It's easy to get discouraged at the outset of a campaign if the gifts you planned on don't materialize. This is especially true when you've laid out a solid strategy and if the people who refused were the very ones who seemed excited and indicated they'd be willing to give.

When this happens, you need to step back from the sting of rejection and take a hard look at the prospects you've called on. How might you have been successful with them – and how can you have a better chance with the prospects that remain?

It may have been the ask itself, or who asked. Or it could have been a circumstance having nothing to do with you (an illness, an unforeseen expense, a drop in corporate revenues). As a first step, go back and ask those who turned you down to tell you why ... *honestly.*

Once you know why your first attempts failed, there are three questions to wrestle with:

• "Will it make a difference to the community if we abandon this program or project?" If not, then it's doubtful your campaign was merited in the first place. You are probably right to give it up.

• "Have we made the case in a compelling way – is it urgent, relevant, and exciting to the community?" If not, then you need to sharpen your message, perhaps using feedback from those who initially rejected you.

• "Do we have other *lead* prospects we can approach, with the goal of engaging them to bring others into the campaign?" If not, then you might postpone your campaign in favor of identifying and cultivating other potential supporters.

Unless there's hard evidence that your campaign is ill-conceived, giving up on it should be a last resort.

38

MISTAKE

You can probably count on a few 'windfall' gifts

The operative word in this mistake is "count on." Early in my career a wise counselor once told me, "Don't expect a miracle, but be ready for it."

We hear about windfall gifts because, like lottery winnings, they're the exception. People like to talk about them. Before long they become legendary.

In truth, there usually *are* a few surprise gifts in most campaigns. They frequently come towards the end – from someone who's been monitoring your progress with interest and wants to be part of your success.

But don't expect any godsends, and don't

inflate your revenue projections.

Instead, you have to plan for every single gift. Compiling lists of potential donors, determining how much they can give, educating them about the organization and drawing them closer to it – these are the underpinnings of successful fundraising.

Yes, *someone* has to win the lottery, as you often hear. Just don't bank on it being you.

39

MISTAKE

Fundraising is a lot easier once you get the hang of it

In some ways, the very act of asking does get easier after a while. You learn what to say, how to handle objections, how to keep the conversation flowing, how to phrase your request for a gift.

But even though asking may become easier, fundraising as a whole remains a daunting task on two levels.

On a personal level, you must continually deal with your own reservations, the ever real possibility of embarrassment, and whatever anxieties you have about rejection. And in spite of years of practice, these concerns may

103

never subside

But fundraising is also daunting on a second, broader level because of what's at stake, namely, your organization and the people who depend on you – sometimes for their very health and well-being. As a result, every solicitation has to be as right as you can make it.

You'll encounter those who claim to love asking and display little hesitation. Perhaps this even describes you. But even here a word of caution is in order.

Never approach fundraising casually. Your success hinges on your knowing as much as possible about your prospective donor – her interests, passions, and needs. That takes time.

Further, you need to be knowledgeable enough about your cause to answer hard questions. Undoubtedly you'll get them.

So if you're getting the hang of asking, savor the feeling. But remember, seasoned professionals look upon each solicitation with a bit of fear and a lot of respect.

As volunteers, we should do the same.

40

MISTAKE

With so many causes raising money, the wells of philanthropy will soon go dry

This in my opinion is a "crutch" mistake – one that says "We didn't succeed because of the competition in our community."

People give according to the things they value and want to see continued in their communities: education, religion, arts, culture, environmental causes. And as long as the organizations they support meet these needs with effective and fiscally sound programs, they will continue to give.

In fact, philanthropy has grown exponentially over the years, keeping pace with the burgeoning number of nonprofits in the U.S. (estimated to be over one million today).

Before declaring the well has run dry – and forsaking the people who rely on you – make sure the dipping bucket is working right. Perhaps you haven't lowered it deep enough to reach the next level of water.

Review the results of your various fundraising efforts. How successful are your events? Mailings? What outreach have you made to donors? Have you marketed the impact of what you're doing? Are you staffed adequately to compete in a crowded marketplace? Are there opportunities for collaboration with similar organizations?

In all likelihood concerns about the wells of philanthropy running dry are simply doubts about your organization's ability to do what's necessary to raise money in today's competitive climate.

A Final Word

"Mistakes are painful when they happen, but years later a collection of mistakes is what is called experience."
–Denis Waitley

This book reflects my experience. These are mistakes I have observed. They are also mistakes I have made.

In working with hundreds of boards and thousands of board members over the years, I have seen all of these and more.

But I have also witnessed the triumph of overcoming these mistakes, and I savor memories of excited calls from those I have coached.

I recall the board member who persuaded her CEO that, yes, they could ask for $1 million from a certain couple, even though others on the board had decided "they probably don't have that kind of money." It literally took less than a minute for the couple to say "yes."

I remember the young man who attended a workshop who realized he had a "widow's mite" donor waiting to be reached out to. He did, and the organization was blessed with a large estate gift.

I know firsthand of organizations that have focused intently on big donors, ignoring the other gifts that comprise philanthropy. I have seen them reeling in times of crisis when others, who had engaged *all* of their donors, were able to keep moving forward.

And I have seen boards, those who longed for a development director to relieve them of fundraising, become even more active advocates, ambassadors, and askers as a result of a skilled professional on staff.

I hope that in this book you have discovered some ideas, truths, and tips that will help you overcome the mistakes and clear the way for your organization to be inordinately successful.

That is my wish, and was my purpose in writing it. Will we continue to make mistakes? Of course. And, we will continue to learn from them as we magnify the impact of our work in philanthropy.

George Soros, whose philanthropy has touched so many, gives us a good parting thought: "Once we realize that imperfect understanding is the human condition, there is no shame in being wrong, only in failing to correct our own mistakes."

THE AUTHOR

Kay Sprinkel Grace is a prolific writer, creative thinker, inspiring speaker, and reflective practitioner. Her passion for philanthropy and its capacity to transform donors, organizations, and communities is well-known in the U.S. and internationally.

With an increasingly powerful vision for the way in which organizations, funders, and communities must partner to resolve community problems and enhance cultural, educational, and other resources, Kay has increased the understanding and motivation of donors and organizations regarding the importance of the philanthropic sector in today's changing and challenging society.

She lives in San Francisco and is an enthusiastic photographer, traveler, hiker and creative writer. When not writing, speaking, or consulting, you can find her with her children and grandchildren who live in San Francisco, upstate New York, and France.

The Triple Crown for Nonprofit Boards

The Ultimate Board Member's Book
A 1-Hour Guide to Understanding and Fulfilling
Your Role and Responsibilities • *Kay Sprinkel Grace*

Here is a book for *all* nonprofit boards.
• Those wanting to operate with maximum effectiveness
• Those needing to clarify exactly what their job is, and,
• Those wanting to ensure that all members – novice and veteran alike – are 'on the same page' with respect to roles and responsibilities.
It's all here in jargon-free language: how boards work, what the job entails, the time commitment, the role of staff, serving on committees, fundraising responsibilities, conflicts of interest, group decision-making, board self-evaluation, and more.

Fund Raising Realities
Every Board Member Must Face
A 1-Hour Crash Course on Raising Major Gifts
for Nonprofit Organizations • *David Lansdowne*

More than 50,000 board members and development officers across America have used the book, *Fund Raising Realities*, to help them raise substantial money – in good *and* bad economies.
In fact, David Lansdowne's classic has become *the* fastest selling fundraising book in America.
It's easy to see why. Have your board spend just one hour with this eyeopening gem and they'll come to understand virtually everything they need to know about raising big gifts.

Asking
A 59-Minute Guide to Everything Board Members,
Volunteers, and Staff Must Know to Secure the Gift
Jerold Panas

It ranks right up there with public speaking. Nearly all of us fear it. And yet it's critical to our success as board members and staff. Asking for money. It makes even the stout-hearted quiver.
But now comes the book, *Asking*, and short of a medical elixir it's the next best thing for emboldening you, your board members, and your volunteers to ask with skill, finesse ... and powerful results.
Nearly everyone, regardless of their persuasive ability, can become an effective fundraiser by following Jerold Panas' step-by-step guidelines.

Order from Emerson & Church, Publishers
508-359-0019 • www.contributionsmagazine.com